SUPER
SANDCASTLE
State Stories

DIXIE'S BIG HEART

~ A Story About Alabama ~

Written by Nancy Tuminelly

Illustrated by Bob Doucet

Consulting Editor, Diane Craig, M.A./Reading Specialist

A Division of ABDO
ABDO
Publishing Company

visit us at www.abdopublishing.com

Published by ABDO Publishing Company, a division of ABDO, P.O. Box 398166, Minneapolis, Minnesota 55439. Copyright © 2011 by Abdo Consulting Group, Inc. International copyrights reserved in all countries. No part of this book may be reproduced in any form without written permission from the publisher. Super SandCastle™ is a trademark and logo of ABDO Publishing Company.

Printed in the United States of America, North Mankato, Minnesota
112010
012011

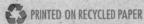 PRINTED ON RECYCLED PAPER

Editor: Liz Salzmann
Content Developer: Nancy Tuminelly
Cover and Interior Design: Anders Hanson, Mighty Media
Production: Colleen Dolphin, Oona Gaarder-Juntti, Mighty Media
Photo Credits: Autiger at en.wikipedia, Dothan Convention and Visitors Bureau, Engbretson Underwater Photography, Getty Images, iStockphoto (Dougal Campbell, Steve Shepard), One Mile Up, Quarter-dollar coin image from the United States Mint, Racking Horse Breeders Association of America, Shutterstock, Phil Thomas/Enterprise Chamber of Commerce, Frank Wadsworth

Library of Congress Cataloging-in-Publication Data

Tuminelly, Nancy, 1952-
  Dixie's big heart : a story about Alabama / Nancy Tuminelly ; illustrated by Bob Doucet.
    p. cm. -- (Fact & fable: state stories)
  ISBN 978-1-61714-680-0
  1. Alabama--Juvenile literature. I. Doucet, Bob, ill. II. Title.
  F326.3.T86 2011
  976.1--dc22
                          2010022165

Super SandCastle™ books are created by a team of professional educators, reading specialists, and content developers around five essential components—phonemic awareness, phonics, vocabulary, text comprehension, and fluency—to assist young readers as they develop reading skills and strategies and increase their general knowledge. All books are written, reviewed, and leveled for guided reading, early reading intervention, and Accelerated Reader® programs for use in shared, guided, and independent reading and writing activities to support a balanced approach to literacy instruction.

TABLE OF CONTENTS

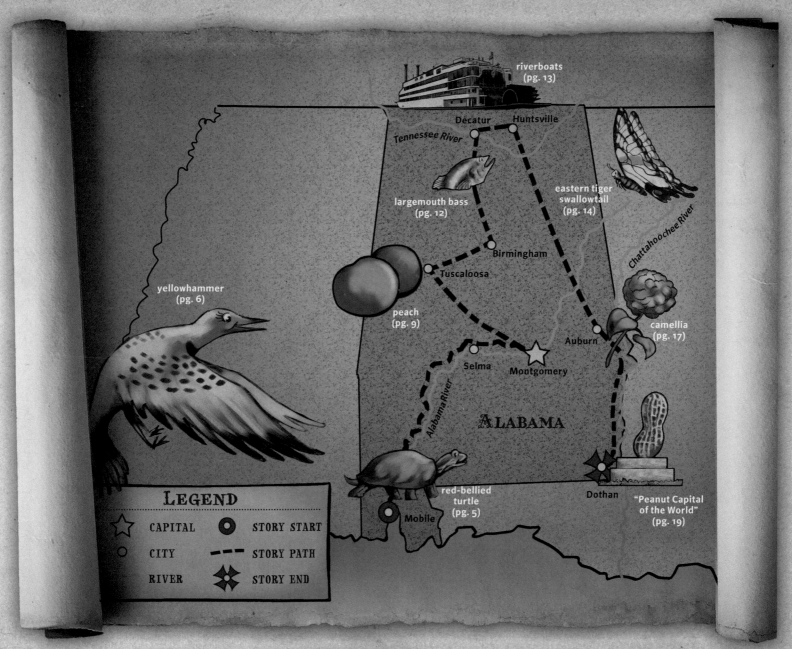

riverboats
(pg. 13)

Decatur   Huntsville

Tennessee River

largemouth bass
(pg. 12)

eastern tiger
swallowtail
(pg. 14)

Chattahoochee River

Birmingham

Tuscaloosa

yellowhammer
(pg. 6)

peach
(pg. 9)

camellia
(pg. 17)

Auburn

Selma   Montgomery

ALABAMA

Alabama River

red-bellied
turtle
(pg. 5)

Dothan

"Peanut Capital
of the World"
(pg. 19)

Mobile

LEGEND

⭐ CAPITAL   ◎ STORY START

◎ CITY   ▬ ▬ STORY PATH

RIVER   ✵ STORY END

Mobile

Mobile is Alabama's only seaport. It's on the Gulf of Mexico at the **delta** of the Mobile River. The Mobile River is formed by the Alabama River and the Tombigbee River. Mobile is the oldest city in Alabama. Civil War battles were fought in Mobile Bay. Mardi Gras began in Mobile.

DIXIE'S BIG HEART

One hot spring day, there was a huge storm in Mobile. The storm came up the delta from the Gulf of Mexico. It rained hard and the rivers flooded. The wind knocked down trees and buildings all over Alabama. After the storm passed, it was quiet.

"What a storm! Good thing it's not Mardi Gras," says Red Belly the turtle.

He digs out from the sand. There are tree branches all over.

"Red Belly, are you okay?" a voice asks. It is Dixie the yellowhammer.

"Yes, Dixie, so nice of you to ask," says Red Belly.

"We had better check on our friends," says Dixie. "Let's start in Montgomery."

Red-Bellied Turtle

The red-bellied turtle is the Alabama state **reptile**. It grows to about 12 inches (30 cm) long. The top shell is green, dark brown, or black. The bottom shell is yellow or red. Red-bellied turtles are only found in Alabama. It lives in the waters of the Mobile **Delta**.

Yellowhammer

The yellowhammer is the Alabama state bird. It has been a **symbol** of Alabama since the Civil War. The yellowhammer is a kind of woodpecker. It is also called a northern flicker. yellowhammers eat more ants than any other bird.

Red Belly and Dixie head up the Alabama River. It is **overflowing** its banks.

They go through Selma. They don't stop until they reach Montgomery, the state capital.

They see the Civil Rights Monument. Everything there is fine. Then they go to the Rosa Parks Library and Museum. There are two broken windows.

"Everyone is safe. It sure is nice of you to check on us," says Miss Mary, the librarian. "Maybe others up north need some help."

Dixie and Red Belly wave good-bye. They are off to see some other friends.

Montgomery

The Alabama State Capitol is a National **Historic** Landmark. Jefferson Davis became the leader of the Confederacy there in 1861. Dr. Martin Luther King Jr. gave a famous speech there in 1965. Other fun things to see are the Montgomery Zoo and Old Alabama Town.

Tuscaloosa

Tuscaloosa is named after a Native American, Chief Tuskaloosa. The **University** of Alabama is there. The university's sports teams are called the Crimson Tide. A big event each year is the football game between Alabama and Auburn University. The game is called the Iron Bowl.

"Thank goodness!" says Dixie as they pass the University of Alabama football **stadium**. "Nothing here was hurt by the storm."

"Who cares? I'm an Auburn fan. Go Tigers!" says Red Belly.

"That's not nice," says Dixie. "Now is not the time to be mean."

Next Dixie and Red Belly go by the peach **orchards**. The storm did not hurt them either.

"These peaches are great. We could make peach cobbler! Let's take some with us. Someone may need food," says Dixie.

"Besides you and me?" asks Red Belly. "Yum!"

"Come on, let's go check on Colonel Davis," says Dixie.

Peach Cobbler

2 cups fresh peaches, peeled and sliced

2 cups sugar

1 cup flour

2 teaspoons baking powder

pinch of salt

1 cup milk

1 stick (½ cup) butter or margarine

Preheat the oven to 350 degrees. Put the peaches and 1 cup sugar in a medium pot. Cook over low heat until the peaches are soft. Stir often. Mix the flour, baking powder, salt, and 1 cup sugar in a bowl. Stir in the milk. Melt the butter in a 9-inch square pan. Pour the flour mixture into the pan. Spoon the peaches on top. Bake for 1 hour. Cool for 15 minutes. Serve warm.

Peach

The peach is the state tree fruit of Alabama. Peaches have been grown in Alabama since 1850. They were made the official tree fruit in 2006. There is a peach **festival** every year in Clanton, Alabama. Clanton also has a peach-shaped water tower!

9

Racking Horse

The racking horse is the Alabama state horse. It is beautiful, smart, and calm. Racking horses are easy to ride for a long time. They have a different **gait** than other horses. Only one foot hits the ground at a time. They have long necks and very smooth hair.

Red Belly and Dixie go toward Birmingham. They pass farms and horse barns. Dixie sees her old friend eating hay.

"Colonel Davis, we came to make sure you're all right," says Dixie. "Want some peach cobbler?"

"Everything is fine, thank you," says Colonel Davis. "I love peaches! You are so kind. Come and visit anytime!"

Then Red Belly and Dixie stop in Birmingham. There are broken trees. But most things look unharmed.

They see their friends at the zoo. "Everyone is fine here," says Kaitlyn the kangaroo. "Thanks for checking on us!"

Their last stop is Vulcan Park. The giant iron statue is safe. Red Belly doesn't really care. He thinks it's scary!

"Let's keep going," says Dixie.

Birmingham

Birmingham is the largest city in Alabama. It's called "The Magic City" because it grew so fast. Birmingham is near the Appalachian Mountains. There are many things to see such as the Birmingham Civil Rights Institute, the Alabama Sports Hall of Fame, the Birmingham Zoo, and Vulcan Park.

Largemouth Bass

The largemouth bass is the Alabama state fish. It eats other fish and crayfish. It can weigh more than 15 pounds (6.8 kg).

They stop at Lewis Smith Lake. "You're a long way from home," says a largemouth bass in the water.

"Hi Larry! We're making sure everyone is all right after the storm. Want some cobbler?" asks Dixie.

"I'm okay, thanks. The water is high. The storm didn't bother me," says Larry, avoiding a fishing line.

Dixie and Red Belly's next stop is Decatur. They see the flooded river. Riverboats are tied to the docks. Then they see the old **historic** houses. Nothing was hurt.

"It's good. Everyone helps each other here," says Dixie. "It's the American way."

"That's why everyone likes Dixie," thinks Red Belly. "She cares about everybody."

Decatur

Decatur is called the "River City." It is on the Tennessee River. Riverboats give tours. Visitors also enjoy the Civil War Walking Tour, the Wheeler National Wildlife Refuge, and the water park at Mallard Park.

13

Eastern Tiger Swallowtail

The eastern tiger swallowtail is the Alabama state butterfly. The male swallowtails are bright yellow with black markings. The female swallowtails are dark. They look like the poisonous pipevine swallowtail. Predators stay away from them.

When they get near Huntsville, they see a bright yellow butterfly. He asks, "Is that you, Dixie?"

"Tiger! I'm glad to see you! We're checking on our friends," says Dixie. "Tiger, meet Red Belly."

"You aren't a tiger," says Red Belly. Red Belly really likes tigers.

"Oh, stop," Dixie says to the turtle.

Tiger goes into Huntsville with Dixie and Red Belly.

"Let's check out the Space and Rocket Center," says Dixie.

Red Belly is excited. He's always wanted to see the rocket that went to the moon. He forgets all about tigers.

"Everything here is good," says Tiger. "Thanks for thinking about us, Dixie. See you again soon!"

Huntsville

Huntsville is known as the "Rocket City." The first rocket that went to the moon was built in Huntsville. The NASA Marshall Space Flight Center and the Redstone Arsenal are also there.

Auburn

Auburn is a southern college town. It is the home of Auburn **University** and the Auburn Tigers sports teams. Auburn is Alabama's largest university. The University sporting events are a big part of the town activities. There are also many parks and lakes to enjoy.

The next stop is Auburn. "Everything here had better be safe," says Red Belly. "Especially the Tigers!"

"Please stop all of that **nonsense**. Just be nice for one day," says Dixie.

"YEAH!" thinks Red Belly when he sees the **stadium** is unharmed. He wonders when the Tigers will play the Crimson Tide again. But he doesn't say a word to Dixie.

"Okay, Dixie, you are right," says Red Belly. "That's why everyone likes you. You're always nice."

The camellias on **campus** are beautiful. The storm didn't harm them.

Red Belly picks a pink bloom. He gives it to Dixie. "This is for you. You always give everything to others," says the turtle.

"That's so nice, Red Belly! Thank you," says Dixie.

Camellia

The camellia is the Alabama state flower. It originally came from China. In the United States, it grows only in the southeast. The flowers can be five inches (12.7 cm) wide. They have round, **overlapping petals** and yellow centers.

17

Southern Longleaf Pine

The southern longleaf pine is the Alabama state tree. A young longleaf pine looks more like grass than a tree. This is because it grows mostly underground for the first five years. Older longleaf pines can be 150 feet (45.7 m) tall.

Dixie and Red Belly go down the Chattahoochee River. It is on the border of Georgia. They see forests of longleaf pine trees.

Some branches are lying on the ground. But no trees are hurt too badly.

Soon, they reach Dothan. It is the "Peanut Capital of the World." The peanut farms are unharmed, too.

"Thanks for asking me to help," says Red Belly. "Everyone was so happy to see you."

"Us!" says Dixie. "They were happy to see both of us. The storm gave us a reason to see our friends. I hope they will help me if I need it. That's what friends are for."

"Let's not wait for another storm to visit again!" says Red Belly.

THE END

Dothan

Dothan is called the "Peanut Capital of the World." There is a giant gold peanut statue at the Visitor's Center. There is also a Dr. George Washington Carver monument. He invented more than 300 uses for peanuts.

ALABAMA AT A GLANCE

Abbreviation: AL

Capital: Montgomery

Largest city: Birmingham

Statehood: December 14, 1819 (22nd state)

Area: 51,700 square miles (133,902 sq km) (30th-largest state)

Nicknames: Cotton State or Yellowhammer State

Motto: Audemus jura nostra defendere — We dare defend our rights

State flower: camellia

State tree: southern longleaf pine

State bird: yellowhammer

State fish: largemouth Bass

State tree fruit: peach

State reptile: red-bellied turtle

State horse: racking horse

State song: "Alabama"

STATE SEAL

STATE FLAG

STATE QUARTER

The Alabama quarter has a picture of Helen Keller. She is reading a book in Braille. Her name is in Braille also. Under her chair is a banner with the slogan, "Spirit of Courage." There are camellias along the right edge of the coin. There are southern longleaf pines along the left edge.

WHAT DO YOU KNOW?

How well do you remember the story? Match the pictures to the
questions below! Then check your answers at the bottom of the page!

a. Larry the largemouth bass

b. University of Alabama football stadium

c. peaches

d. racking horse

e. yellowhammer

f. camellia

1. What kind of animal is Dixie?

2. What do Dixie and Red Belly pass in Tuscaloosa?

3. What kind of fruit do Dixie and Red Belly eat?

4. What kind of animal is Colonel Davis?

5. Who do Dixie and Red Belly meet at Lewis Smith Lake?

6. What does Red Belly give to Dixie?

What to Do in Alabama

1 **Explore a Prehistoric Cave!**
Russell Cave, Bridgeport

2 **Hike to the Highest point in Alabama**
Cheaha Mountain, Lineville

3 **See a Crater Made by a Meteor!**
Wetumpka Impact Crater, Elmore County

4 **Travel a Historic Trail**
Selma to Montgomery National Historic Trail, Selma

5 **Eat Great Barbecue!**
Christmas on the River Barbecue Cook-off contest, Demopolis

6 **Play on White Sand Beaches**
Gulf of Mexico Shoreline, Gulf Shores

7 **Learn How Boll Weevils Ruined the Cotton Crop**
Giant boll weevil statue, Enterprise

8 **Visit a Museum!**
George Washington Carver Museum, Tuskegee

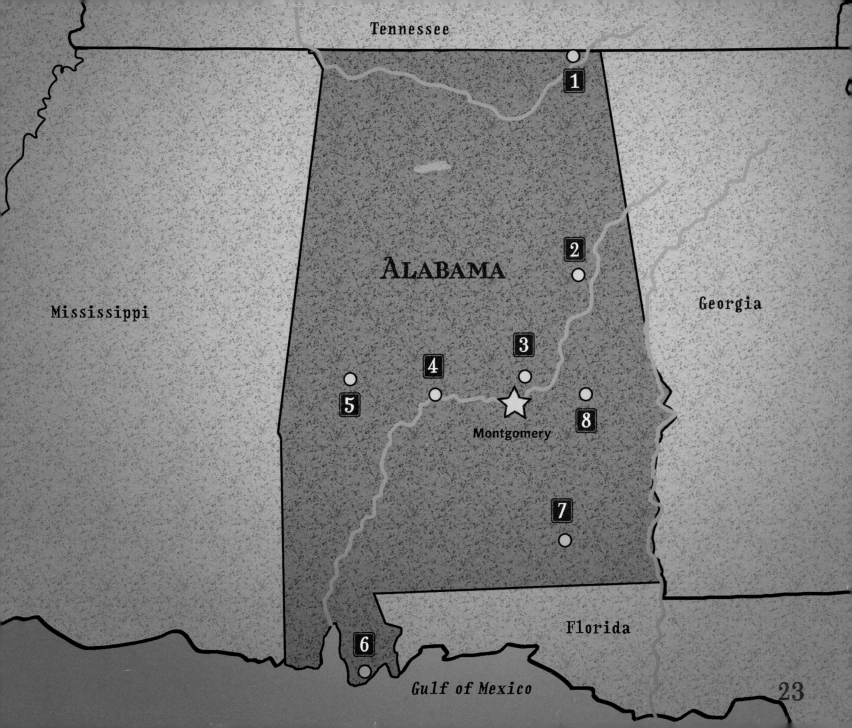

Tennessee

1

Mississippi

ALABAMA

2

Georgia

3

4

5

8

☆
Montgomery

7

6

Florida

Gulf of Mexico

GLOSSARY

campus – the buildings and land that make up a college or school.

delta – an area of land where a river spreads out before entering the sea.

festival – a celebration that happens at the same time each year.

gait – the way a person or animal walks or runs.

historic – being an important or famous part of history.

nonsense – an idea, behavior, or statement that is foolish, silly, or annoying.

orchard – a place where fruit or nut trees are grown.

overflow – to spill over the top.

overlap – to lie partly on top of something.

petal – one of the thin, colored parts of a flower.

reptile – a cold-blooded animal, such as a snake, turtle, or alligator, that moves on its belly or on very short legs.

stadium – a large building with an open area for sporting events surrounded by rows of seats.

symbol – an object that stands for or represents something else.

university – a large school you go to after finishing high school. A university is often made up of several colleges.